My Visit to the Doctor

Rachel Tisdale

Photography by Chris Fairclough

W

First published in 2007 by
Franklin Watts
338 Euston Road
London NW1 3BH

Franklin Watts Australia
Level 17/207 Kent Street
Sydney NSW 2000

ISBN: 978 0 7496 7455 7 (hbk)
ISBN: 978 0 7496 7467 0 (pbk)

Dewey classification number: 610.69

A CIP catalogue record for this book is available from the British Library.

Planning and production by Discovery Books Limited
Editor: James Nixon
Designer: Ian Winton
Photography: Chris Fairclough
Series advisors: Diana Bentley MA and Dee Reid MA,
Fellows of Oxford Brookes University

The author, packager and publisher would like to thank the following
people for their participation in this book: Arran and Kam Bola, Diane Payne
and the staff at Quinborne Medical Practice.

All photographs by Chris Fairclough.

Printed in China

Franklin Watts is a division of Hachette Children's books,
an Hachette Livre UK company.

Contents

Feeling unwell

Arran has earache.
He has to visit the
doctor.

Mum makes an appointment.

The surgery

Mum and Arran arrive at the surgery.

The waiting room

Arran waits to see
the doctor.

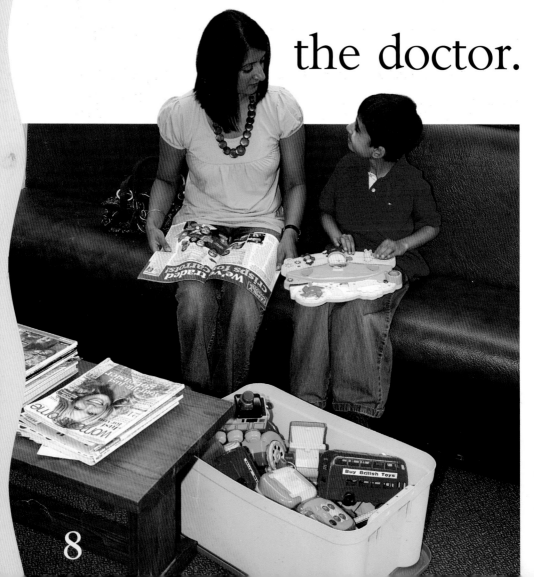

The doctor rings the bell.

You can go in now.

Ear infection

The doctor looks
inside Arran's ear.

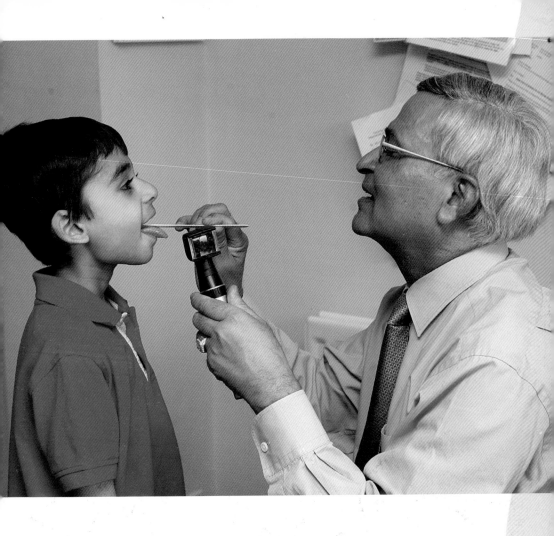

Then he checks
Arran's throat.

A prescription

Arran needs some medicine. The doctor prints a prescription.

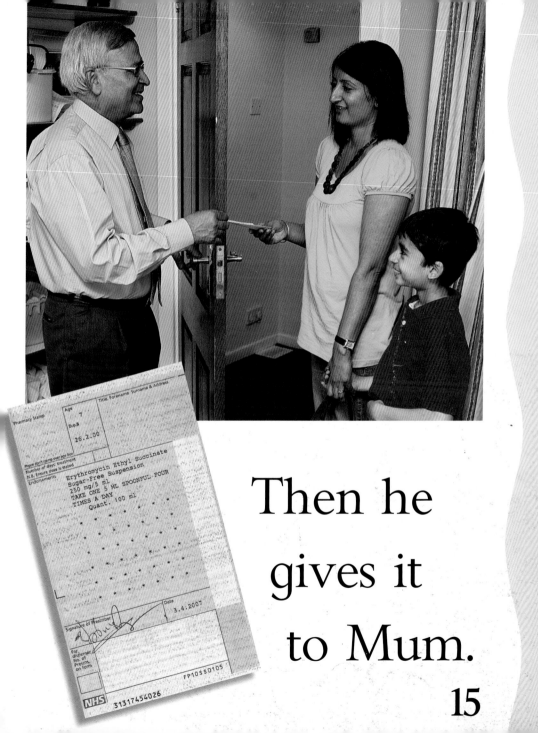

Then he gives it to Mum.

Leaving the surgery

Mum and Arran leave the surgery.

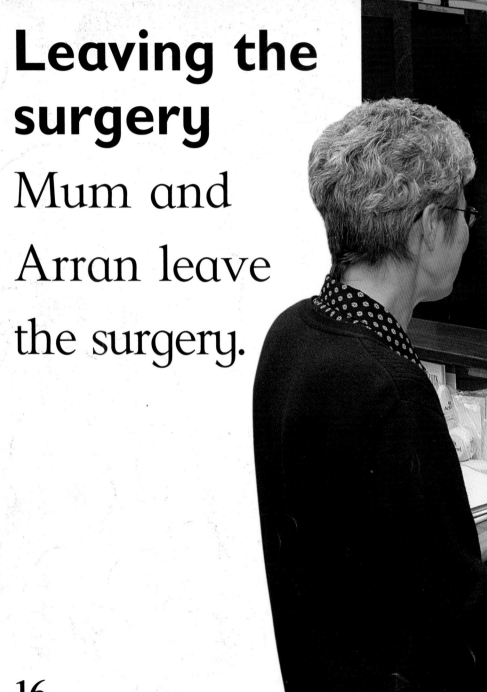

The pharmacy

Mum and Arran go to the pharmacy to get Arran's medicine.

Mum gives the prescription to the assistant.

Medicine

The chemist finds the right medicine for Arran.

Feeling better

Arran takes his medicine every day.

Soon he feels
much better.

Word bank

Look back for these words and pictures.

Assistant

Chemist

Doctor

Earache

Medicine

Pharmacy

Prescription

Surgery

Waiting room